BOOKS BY MICHAEL ONDAATJE

PROSE

Coming through Slaughter (1976)

Running in the Family (memoir) (1982)

In the Skin of a Lion (1987)

The English Patient (1992)

POETRY

The Dainty Monsters (1967)

The Man with 7 Toes (1969)

The Collected Works of Billy the Kid (1970)

Rat Jelly (1973)

Elimination Dance (1976)

There's a Trick with a Knife I'm Learning to Do (1979)

Tin Roof (1982)

Secular Love (1984)

The Cinnamon Peeler (1992)

Handwriting (1998)

ANTHOLOGIES

The Long Poem Anthology (1967)

From Ink Lake: Canadian Stories (1991)

The Brick Reader (with Linda Spalding) (1991)

HANDWRITING

Michael Ondaatje

POEMS

HANDWRITING

Alfred A. Knopf   *New York 1999*

THIS IS A BORZOI BOOK
PUBLISHED BY ALFRED A. KNOPF, INC.

Copyright © 1998 by Michael Ondaatje

All rights reserved under International and Pan-American Copyright
Conventions. Published in the United States by Alfred A. Knopf, Inc.,
New York. Distributed by Random House, Inc., New York.

www.randomhouse.com

Originally published in Canada by McClelland & Stewart Inc.,
Toronto, in 1998.

Knopf, Borzoi Books, and the colophon are registered trademarks
of Random House, Inc.

Library of Congress Cataloging-in-Publication Data

Ondaatje, Michael, [date]
    Handwriting : poems / by Michael Ondaatje.—1st ed.
        p.   cm.
    ISBN 0-375-40559-3.
        1. Sri Lankans—Canada—Poetry.   2. Sri Lanka—Poetry.   I. Title
PR9199.3.05H36   1999
811'.54—dc21
                                                        98-41731
                                                            CIP

Manufactured in the United States of America
First United States Edition

for Rosalin Perera

"For the long nights you lay awake
And watched for my unworthy sake:
For your most comfortable hand
That led me through the uneven land . . ."

CONTENTS

1

A Gentleman Compares His Virtue
to a Piece of Jade

The enemy was always identified in art by a lion.

And in our Book of Victories
wherever you saw a parasol
on the battlefield you could
identify the king within its shadow.

We began with myths and later included actual events.

There were new professions. Cormorant Girls
who screamed on prawn farms to scare birds.
Stilt-walkers. Tightrope-walkers.

There was always the "untaught hold"
by which the master defeated
the pupil who challenged him.

Palanquins carried the weapons of a goddess.

Bamboo tubes cut in 17th-century Japan
we used as poem holders.

We tied bells onto falcons.

A silted water garden in Mihintale.
The letter *M*. The word "thereby."

There were wild cursive scripts.
There was the two-dimensional tradition.

Solitaries spent all their years
writing one good book. Federico Tesio
graced us with *Breeding the Race Horse*.

In our theatres human beings
wondrously became other human beings.

Bangles from Polonnaruwa.
A nine-chambered box from Gampola.
The archaeology of cattle bells.

We believed in the intimate life, an inner self.

A libertine was one who made love before nightfall
or without darkening the room.

Walking the Alhambra blindfolded
to be conscious of the sound of water—your hand
could feel it coursing down banisters.

We aligned our public holidays with the full moon.

3 a.m. in temples, the hour of washing the gods.

The formalization of the vernacular.

The Buddha's left foot shifted at the moment of death.

That great writer, dying, called out
for the fictional doctor in his novels.

That tightrope-walker from Kurunegala
the generator shut down by insurgents

stood there
swaying in the darkness above us.

The Distance of a Shout

We lived on the medieval coast
south of warrior kingdoms
during the ancient age of the winds
as they drove all things before them.

Monks from the north came
down our streams floating—that was
the year no one ate river fish.

There was no book of the forest,
no book of the sea, but these
are the places people died.

Handwriting occurred on waves,
on leaves, the scripts of smoke,
a sign on a bridge along the Mahaweli River.

A gradual acceptance of this new language.

Buried

To be buried in times of war,
in harsh weather, in the monsoon
of knives and stakes.

The stone and bronze gods carried
during a night rest of battle
between the sleeping camps
floated in catamarans down the coast
past Kalutara.
                        To be buried
for safety.

To bury, surrounded by flares,
large stone heads
during floods in the night.
Dragged from a temple
by one's own priests,
lifted onto palanquins,
covered with mud and straw.
Giving up the sacred
among themselves,
carrying the faith of a temple
during political crisis
away in their arms.
                        Hiding
the gestures of the Buddha.

Above ground, massacre and race.
A heart silenced.
The tongue removed.
The human body merged into burning tire.
Mud glaring back
into a stare.

*

750 AD the statue of a Samadhi Buddha
was carefully hidden, escaping war,
the treasure hunters, fifty-year feuds.
He was discovered by monks in 1968
sitting upright
buried in Anuradhapura earth,
eyes half closed, hands
in the gesture of meditation.

Pulled from the earth with ropes
into a surrounding world.
Pulled into heatwave, insect noise,
bathers splashing in tanks.

Bronze became bronze
around him,
colour became colour.

*

In the heart of the forest, the faith.

Stone columns. Remnants of a dagoba
in this clearing torn out of jungle.

No human image remains.

What is eternal is brick, stone,
a black lake where water disappears
below mud and rises again,
the arc of the dagoba that echoes a mountain.

Bo Tree. Chapter House. Image House.

A line of stones
the periphery of sleeping quarters
for 12th-century monks,

their pocket of faith
buried away from the world.

Dusk. The grass and stone blue.
Black lake.
Seven hundred years ago
a saffron scar of monks
moving in the clearing
and at this hour the sky
almost saffron.
                    A saffron bird.
In the bowl of rice, a saffron seed.

They are here for two hundred years.

When war reaches them
they carry the statues deeper
into jungle and vanish.
The pocket is sewn shut.

Where water sinks
lower than mud, they dig
and bury the sacred
then hide beyond
this black lake
that reappears and
disappears. A lake unnamed
save for its colour.

The lost monks
who are overtaken or are silent
the rest of their lives,
who fade away thin
as the skeletons of leaf.

Fifteen generations later armed men hide
in the jungles, trapping animals,
plucking the crimson leaf to boil it
or burn it or smoke it.
Sects of war.
                    A hundred beliefs.

Men carrying recumbent Buddhas

or men carrying mortars
burning the enemy, disappearing
into pits when they hear helicopters.
Girls with poison necklaces
to save themselves from torture.
Just as women wear amulets
which hold their rolled-up fortunes
transcribed on ola leaf.

The statue the weight
of a cannon barrel,
bruising the naked shoulder as they run,
hoisted to a ledge,
then lowered by rope
into another dug pit.

Burying the Buddha in stone.

Covered with soft earth
then the corpse of an animal,

planting a seed there.

                    So roots
like the fingers of a blind monk
spread for two hundred years over his face.

                    *

Night fever

Overlooking a lake
that has buried a village

Bent over a table
shaking from fever
listening for the drowned
name of a town

There's water in my bones
a ghost of a chance

Rock paintings eaten
by amoebic bacteria
streets and temples
that shake within
cliffs of night water

Someone with fever
buried
in the darkness of a room

        *

Lightning over that drowned valley
Thomas Merton who died of electricity

But if I had to perish twice?

The Brother Thief

Four men steal the bronze
Buddha at Veheragala
and disappear from their families

The statue carried
along jungle pathways
its right arm raised
to the jerking sky
in the gesture of
"protection" "reassurance"

towards clouds and birdcall
to this quick terror
in the four men
moving under him

The Buddha with them
all night by a small
thorn fire, touching
the robe at his shoulder,
vitarka mudra—"gesture
of calling for a discourse."
Three of the men asleep.
The youngest feeds the fire
beside the bronze,
allows himself honey
as night progresses
as sounds quiet and thicken,

the shift during night hours
to lesser more various animals.
Creatures like us, he thinks.

Beyond this pupil of heat
all geography is burned

No mountain or star
no river noise,
                nothing
to give him course.

His world is
a honey pot
a statue on its side
the gaze restless
from firelight

      He climbs
behind the bronze
slides his arm around
with the knife
and removes the eyes

      chipped gems
fall into his hands

      then startles
innocent
out of his nightmare

rubs his own eyes

He stands and
breathes night

air deep
into himself

swallows all
he can of
thorn-smoke

nine small sounds
a distant coolness

   Dark peace,
like a cave of water

To Anuradhapura

In the dry lands

every few miles, moving north,
another roadside Ganesh

Straw figures
on bamboo scaffolds
to advertise a family
of stilt-walkers

Men twenty feet high
walking over fields
crossing the thin road
with their minimal arms
and "lying legs"

A dance of tall men
with the movement of prehistoric birds
in practice before they alight

So men become gods
in the small village
of Ilukwewa

Ganesh in pink,
            in yellow,
in elephant darkness

His simplest shrine
a drawing of him

lime chalk
on a grey slate

All this glory
preparing us for Anuradhapura

its night faith

A city with the lap
and spell of a river

Families below trees
around the heart of a fire

tributaries
from the small villages
of the dry zone

Circling the dagoba
in a clockwise hum and chant,
bowls of lit coal
above their heads

whispering bare feet

Our flutter and drift
in the tow of this river

**The First Rule
of Sinhalese
Architecture**

Never build three doors
in a straight line

A devil might rush
through them
deep into your house,
into your life

The Medieval Coast

A village of stone-cutters. A village of soothsayers.
Men who burrow into the earth in search of gems.

Circus in-laws who pyramid themselves into trees.

Home life. A fear of distance along the southern coast.

Every stone-cutter has his secret mark, angle of his chisel.

In the village of soothsayers
bones of a familiar animal
guide interpretations.

This wisdom extends no more than thirty miles.

Buried 2

i

We smuggled the tooth of the Buddha
from temple to temple for five hundred years,
1300–1800.

Once we buried our libraries
under the great medicinal trees
which the invaders burned
—when we lost the books,
the poems of science, invocations.

The tooth picked from the hot loam
and hidden in our hair and buried again
within the rapids of a river.

When they left we swam down to it
and carried it away in our hair.

ii

By the 8th century our rough harbours
had already drowned Persian ships

We drove cylinders into the earth
to discover previous horizons

In the dry zone we climbed great rocks
and rose out of the landscape

Where we saw forests
the king saw water gardens

an ordered river's path circling
and falling,

      he could almost see
the silver light of it
come rushing towards us

iii

The poets wrote their stories on rock and leaf
to celebrate the work of the day,
the shadow pleasures of night.
Kanakara, they said.
Tharu piri . . .

They slept, famous, in palace courtyards
then hid within forests when they were hunted
for composing the arts of love and science
while there was war to celebrate.

They were revealed in their darknesses
—as if a torch were held above the night sea
exposing the bodies of fish—
and were killed and made more famous.

iv

What we lost.

The interior love poem
the deeper levels of the self
landscapes of daily life

dates when the abandonment
of certain principles occurred.

The rule of courtesy—how to enter
a temple or forest, how to touch
a master's feet before lesson or performance.

The art of the drum. The art of eye-painting.
How to cut an arrow. Gestures between lovers.
The pattern of her teeth marks on his skin
drawn by a monk from memory.

The limits of betrayal. The five ways
a lover could mock an ex-lover.

Nine finger and eye gestures
to signal key emotions.

The small boats of solitude.

Lyrics that rose
from love
back into the air

naked with guile
and praise.

Our works and days.

We knew how monsoons
(south-west, north-east)
would govern behaviour

and when to discover
the knowledge of the dead

hidden in clouds,
in rivers, in unbroken rock.

All this we burned or traded for power and wealth
from the eight compass points of vengeance

from the two levels of envy

v

In the forest of kings

a Dilo Oil tree, a Pig Lily,
a Blue Dawn Bonnet flower

Parrot trees. Pigeon Berries.

Alstonia for the making of matchsticks
Twigs of Moonamal for the cleaning of teeth

The Ola leaf on which to compose
our stanzas of faith

Indigo for eyelids, aerograms

The mid-rib of a coconut palm
to knit a fence

Also Kalka, Churna,
Dasamula, Tharalasara . . .

In the south most violence began
over the ownership of trees,

boundary lines—the fruit
and where it fell

Several murders over one jak fruit tree

vi

For years the President built nothing but clock-towers.

The main causes of death
were "extra-judicial execution"
and "exemplary killings."

> *"A woman said a man pretending to be from the*
> *military made her part with four jak trees in*
> *her garden as a consideration for obtaining the*
> *release of her son arrested some years earlier*
> *during the period of terror."*
>
> *Daily News 15.10.94*

The address of torture was off the Galle Road in Kollupitiya

There were goon squads from all sides

Our archaeologists dug down to the disappeared
bodies of schoolchildren

vii

The heat of explosions
sterilized all metal.

Ball bearings and nails
in the arms, in the head.
Shrapnel in the feet.

Ear channels
deformed by shockwaves.
Men without balance
surrounding the dead President
on Armour Street.

Those whose bodies
could not be found.

"All those poets as famous as kings"

Hora gamanak yana ganiyak	A woman who journeys to a tryst
kanakara nathuva	having no jewels,
kaluwan kes kalamba	darkness in her hair,
tharu piri ahasa	the sky lovely with its stars

2

THE NINE SENTIMENTS

(Historical Illustrations on Rock and Book and Leaf)

i

All day desire
enters the hearts of men

Women from the village of _____
move along porches
wearing calling bells

Breath from the mouth
of that moon

Arrows of flint
in their hair

ii

She stands in the last daylight
of the bedroom painting her eye,
holding a small mirror

The brush of sandalwood along the collarbone

Green dark silk

A shoe left
on the cadju tree terrace

these nights when "pools are
reduced by constant plungings"

Meanwhile a man's burning heart
his palate completely dry
on the Galapitigala Road

thinking there is water in that forest

iii

Sidelong coquetry
at the Colombo Apothecary

Desire in sunlight

Aliganaya—"the embrace
during an intoxicated walk"
or "sudden arousal
while driving over speed bumps"

Kissing the birthmark
on a breast,
tugging his lotus stalk
(the literal translation)
on Edith Grove

Or "conquered on a car seat"
along Amarasekera Mawatha

One sees these fires
from a higher place
on the cadju terrace

they wander like gold
ragas of longing
like lit sequin
on her shifting green dress

iv

States of confusion as a result
of the movement of your arm
or your hidden grin

The king's elephants
have left for war
crossing the rivers

His guards loiter in the dark corridors
full of chirping insects

My path to this meeting
was lit by lightning

Your laughter with its
intake of breath. *Uhh huh.*

Kadamba branches driven
by storm into the bedroom

Your powdered anus
your hair on my stomach
releasing its heavy arrow

v

The curve of the bridge
against her foot

her thin shadow falling
through slats
into water movement

A woman and her echo

The kessara blossom she kicks
in passing that flowers

You stare into the mirror
that held her painted eye

Ancient dutiful ants
hiding in the ceremonial
yak-tail fan
move towards and climb
her bone of ankle

The Bhramarah bee is drunk
from the south pasture

this insect that has
the letter "r" twice
in its name

vi

Five poems without mentioning the river prawn.

vii

The women of Boralesgamuwa
uproot lotus in mid-river
skin reddened by floating pollen

Songs to celebrate the washing
of arms and bangles

This laughter when husbands are away

An uncaught prawn hiding by their feet

The three folds on their stomachs
considered a sign of beauty

They try out all their ankle bracelets
during these afternoons

viii

The pepper vine shaken and shaken
like someone in love

Leaf patterns

saffron and panic seed
on the lower pillows
where their breath met

while she loosened
from her hips the string
with three calling bells

her fearless heart
light as a barn owl
against him all night

ix

An old book on the poisons
of madness, a map
of forest monasteries,
a chronicle brought across
the sea in Sanskrit slokas.
I hold all these
but you have become
a ghost for me.

I hold only your shadow
since those days I drove
your nature away.

A falcon who became a coward.

I hold you the way astronomers
draw constellations for each other
in the markets of wisdom

placing shells
on a dark blanket
saying "these
are the heavens"

calculating the movement
of the great stars

x

Walking through rainstorms to a tryst,
the wet darkness of her aureoles

the Sloka, the Pada, the secret Rasas

the curved line of her shadow

the Vasanta-Tilaka or Upajati metres

bare feet down ironwood stairs

A confluence now
of her eyes,
her fingers, her teeth
as she tightens the hood
over the gaze of a falcon

Love arrives and dies in all disguises
and we fear to move
because of old darknesses
or childhood danger

So our withdrawing words
our skating hearts

xi

Life before desire,
without conscience.
Cities without rivers or bells.

Where is the forest
not cut down
for profit or literature

whose blossoms instead
will close the heart

Where is the suitor
undistressed
one can talk with

Where is there a room
without the damn god of love?

3

Flight

In the half-dark cabin of Air Lanka Flight 5
the seventy-year-old lady next to me begins to comb
her long white hair, then braids it in the faint light.

Her husband, Mr Jayasinghe, asleep beside her.

Pins in her mouth. She rolls her hair,
curls it into a bun, like my mother's.

Two hours before reaching Katunayake airport.

Wells

i

The rope jerked up
so the bucket flies
into your catch

pours over you

its moment
of encasement

standing in sunlight
wanting more,
another poem please

and each time
recognition and caress,
the repeated pleasure

of finite things.
Hypnotized by lyric.
This year's kisses

like diving a hundred times
from a moving train
into the harbour

like diving a hundred times
from a moving train
into the harbour

ii

The last Sinhala word I lost
was *vatura*.
The word for water.
Forest water. The water in a kiss. The tears
I gave to my ayah Rosalin on leaving
the first home of my life.

More water for her than any other
that fled my eyes again
this year, remembering her,
a lost almost-mother in those years
of thirsty love.

No photograph of her, no meeting
since the age of eleven,
not even knowledge of her grave.

Who abandoned who, I wonder now.

iii

In the sunless forest
of Ritigala

heat in the stone
heat in the airless black shadows

nine soldiers on leave
strip uniforms off
and dig a well

to give thanks
for surviving this war

A puja in an unnamed grove
the way someone you know
might lean forward
and mark the place
where your soul is
—always, they say,
near to a wound.

In the sunless forest
crouched by a forest well

pulling what was lost
out of the depth.

The Siyabaslakara

In the 10th century, the young princess
entered a rock pool like the moon

within a blue cloud

Her sisters
who dove, lit by flares,
were lightning

Water and erotics

The path from the king to rainmaking

—his dark shoulders a platform
against the youngest instep

waving her head above him
this way
this way

Later the art of aqueducts,

the banning of monks
from water events

so they would not be caught
within the melodious sounds

or in the noon heat
under the rain of her hair

**Driving with Dominic
in the Southern Province
We See Hints of the Circus**

The tattered Hungarian tent

A man washing a trumpet
at a roadside tap

Children in the trees,

one falling
into the grip of another

Death at Kataragama

For half the day blackouts stroke this house into stillness so there is no longer a whirring fan or the hum of light. You hear sounds of a pencil being felt for in a drawer in the dark and then see its thick shadow in candlelight, writing the remaining words. Paragraphs reduced to one word. A punctuation mark. Then another word, complete as a thought. The way someone's name holds terraces of character, contains all of our adventures together. I walk the corridors which might perhaps, I'm not sure, be cooler than the rest of the house. Heat at noon. Heat in the darkness of night.

There is a woodpecker I am enamoured of I saw this morning through my binoculars. A red thatch roof to his head more modest than crimson, deeper than blood. Distance is always clearer. I no longer see words in focus. As if my soul is a blunt tooth. I bend too close to the page to get nearer to what is being understood. What I write will drift away. I will be able to understand the world only at arm's length.

Can my soul step into the body of that woodpecker? He may be too hot in sunlight, it could be a limited life. But if this had been offered to me today, at 9 a.m., I would have gone with him, traded this body for his.

A constant fall of leaf around me in this time of no rain like the continual habit of death. Someone soon will say of me, "his body was lying in Kataragama like a pauper." Vanity even when we are a corpse. For a blue hand that contains no touch or desire in it for another.

There is something else. Not just the woodpecker. Ten water buffalo when I stopped the car. They were being veered from side to side under the sun. The sloshing of their hooves in the paddy field that I heard thirty yards away, my car door open for the breeze, the haunting sound I was caught within as if creatures of magnificence were undressing and removing their wings. My head and almost held breath out there for an hour so that later I felt as if I contained that full noon light.

It was water in an earlier life I could not take into my mouth when I was dying. I was soothed then the way a plant would be, brushed with a wet cloth, as I reduced all thought into requests. Take care of this flower. Less light. Curtain. As I lay there prone during the long vigil of my friends. The ache of ribs from too much sleep or fever—bones that protect the heart and breath in battle, during love beside another. Saliva, breath, fluids, the soul. The place bodies meet is the place of escape.

But this time brutal aloneness. The straight stern legs of the woodpecker braced against the jak fruit as he delves for a meal. Will he feel the change in his nature as my soul enters? Will it go darker? Or will I enter as I always do another's nest, in their clothes and with their rules for a particular life.

Or I could leap into knee-deep mud potent with rice. Ten water buffalo. A quick decision. Not goals considered all our lives but, in the final minutes, sudden choice. This morning it was a woodpecker. A year ago the face of someone on a train. We depart into worlds that have nothing to do with those we love. This woman whose arm I would hold and comfort, that book I wanted to make and shape tight as a stone—I would give everything away for this sound of mud and water, hooves, great wings

The Great Tree

"Zou Fulei died like a dragon breaking down a wall . . .

this line composed and ribboned
in cursive script
by his friend the poet Yang Weizhem

whose father built a library
surrounded by hundreds of plum trees

It was Zou Fulei, almost unknown,
who made the best plum flower painting
of any period

One branch lifted into the wind

and his friend's vertical line of character

their tones of ink
—wet to opaque
dark to pale

each sweep and gesture
trained and various
echoing the other's art

In the high plum-surrounded library
where Yang Weizhem studied as a boy

a moveable staircase was pulled away
to ensure his solitary concentration

His great work
"untrammelled" "eccentric" "unorthodox"
"no taint of the superficial"
    "no flamboyant movement"

using at times the lifted tails
of archaic script,

sharing with Zou Fulei
his leaps and darknesses

    *

"So I have always held you in my heart . . .

The great 14th-century poet calligrapher
mourns the death of his friend

Language attacks the paper from the air

There is only a path of blossoms

no flamboyant movement

A night of smoky ink in 1361
a night without a staircase

The Story

i

For his first forty days a child
is given dreams of previous lives.
Journeys, winding paths,
a hundred small lessons
and then the past is erased.

Some are born screaming,
some full of introspective wandering
into the past—that bus ride in winter,
the sudden arrival within
a new city in the dark.
And those departures from family bonds
leaving what was lost and needed.
So the child's face is a lake
of fast moving clouds and emotions.

A last chance for the clear history of the self.
All our mothers and grandparents here,
our dismantled childhoods
in the buildings of the past.

Some great forty-day daydream
before we bury the maps.

ii

There will be a war, the king told his pregnant wife.
In the last phase seven of us will cross
the river to the east and disguise ourselves
through the farmlands.
We will approach the markets
and befriend the rope-makers. Remember this.

She nods and strokes the baby in her belly.

After a month we will enter
the halls of that king.
There is dim light from small high windows.
We have entered with no weapons,
just rope in the baskets.
We have trained for years
to move in silence, invisible,
not one creak of bone,
not one breath,
even in lit rooms,
in order to disappear into this building
where the guards live in half-light.

When a certain night falls
the seven must enter the horizontal door
remember this, face down,
as in birth.

Then (he tells his wife)
there is the corridor of dripping water,
a noisy rain, a sense
of creatures at your feet.
And we enter halls of further darkness,
cold and wet among the enemy warriors.
To overcome them we douse the last light.

After battle we must leave another way
avoiding all doors to the north . . .

(The king looks down
and sees his wife is asleep
in the middle of the adventure.

He bends down and kisses through the skin
the child in the body of his wife.
Both of them in dreams. He lies there,
watches her face as it catches a breath.
He pulls back a wisp across her eye
and bites it off. Braids it
into his own hair, then sleeps beside them.)

iii

With all the swerves of history
I cannot imagine your future.
Would wish to dream it, see you
in your teens, as I saw my son,
your already philosophical air
rubbing against the speed of the city.
I no longer guess a future.
And do not know how we end
nor where.

Though I know a story about maps, for you.

iv

After the death of his father,
the prince leads his warriors
into another country.
Four men and three women.
They disguise themselves and travel
through farms, fields of turnip.
They are private and shy
in an unknown, uncaught way.

In the hemp markets
they court friends.
They are dancers who tumble
with lightness as they move,
their long hair wild in the air.
Their shyness slips away.

They are charming with desire in them.
It is the dancing they are known for.

One night they leave their beds.
Four men, three women.
They cross open fields where nothing grows
and swim across the cold rivers
into the city.

Silent, invisible among the guards,
they enter the horizontal door

face down so the blades of poison
do not touch them. Then
into the rain of the tunnels.

It is an old story—that one of them
remembers the path in.
They enter the last room of faint light
and douse the lamp. They move
within the darkness like dancers
at the centre of a maze
seeing the enemy before them
with the unlit habit of their journey.

There is no way to behave after victory.

          *

And what should occur now is unremembered.

The seven stand there.
One among them, who was that baby,
cannot recall the rest of the story
—the story his father knew, unfinished
that night, his mother sleeping.

We remember it as a tender story,
though perhaps they perish.
The father's lean arm across
the child's shape, the taste
of the wisp of hair in his mouth . . .

The seven embrace in the destroyed room
where they will die without
the dream of exit.
We do not know what happened.
From the high windows the ropes
are not long enough to reach the ground.
They take up the knives of the enemy
and cut their long hair and braid it
onto one rope and they descend
hoping it will be long enough
into the darkness of the night.

House on a Red Cliff

There is no mirror in Mirissa

the sea is in the leaves
the waves are in the palms

old languages in the arms
of the casuarina pine
parampara

parampara, from
generation to generation

The flamboyant a grandfather planted
having lived through fire
lifts itself over the roof

unframed

the house an open net

where the night concentrates
on a breath
            on a step
a thing or gesture
we cannot be attached to

The long, the short, the difficult minutes
of night

where even in darkness
there is no horizon without a tree

just a boat's light in the leaves

Last footstep before formlessness

Step

The ceremonial funeral structure for a monk
made up of thambili palms, white cloth
is only a vessel, disintegrates

completely as his life.

The ending disappears,
replacing itself

with something abstract
as air, a view.

All we'll remember in the last hours
is an afternoon—a lazy lunch
then sleeping together.

Then the disarray of grief.

    *

On the morning of a full moon
in a forest monastery
thirty women in white
meditate on the precepts of the day
until darkness.

They walk those abstract paths
their complete heart
their burning thought focused
on this step, then *this* step.

In the red brick dusk
of the Sacred Quadrangle,
among holy seven-storey ambitions
where the four Buddhas
of Polonnaruwa
face out to each horizon,
is a lotus pavilion.

Taller than a man
nine lotus stalks of stone
stand solitary in the grass,
pillars that once supported
the floor of another level.

(The sensuous stalk
the sacred flower)

How physical yearning
became permanent.
How desire became devotional
so it held up your house,
your lover's house, the house of your god.

And though it is no longer there,
the pillars once let you step
to a higher room
where there was worship, lighter air.

Last Ink

In certain countries aromas pierce the heart and one dies
half waking in the night as an owl and a murderer's cart go by

the way someone in your life will talk out love and grief
then leave your company laughing.

In certain languages the calligraphy celebrates
where you met the plum blossom and moon by chance

—the dusk light, the cloud pattern,
recorded always in your heart

and the rest of the world—chaos,
circling your winter boat.

Night of the Plum and Moon.

Years later you shared it
on a scroll or nudged
the ink onto stone
to hold the vista of a life.

A condensary of time in the mountains
—your rain-swollen gate, a summer
scarce with human meeting.
Just bells from another village.

The memory of a woman walking down stairs.

*

Life on an ancient leaf
or a crowded 5th-century seal

this mirror-world of art
—lying on it as if a bed.

When you first saw her,
the night of moon and plum,
you could speak of this to no one.
You cut your desire
against a river stone.
You caught yourself
in a cicada-wing rubbing,
lightly inked.
The indelible darker self.

A seal, the Masters said,
must contain bowing and leaping,
"and that which hides in waters."

Yellow, drunk with ink,
the scroll unrolls to the west
a river journey, each story
an owl in the dark, its child-howl

unreachable now
—that father and daughter,
that lover walking naked down blue stairs
each step jarring the humming from her mouth.

I want to die on your chest but not yet,
she wrote, sometime in the 13th century
of our love

before the yellow age of paper

before her story became a song,
lost in imprecise reproductions

until caught in jade,

whose spectrum could hold the black greens
the chalk-blue of her eyes in daylight.

*

Our altering love, our moonless faith.

Last ink in the pen.

My body on this hard bed.

The moment in the heart
where I roam restless, searching

74

for the thin border of the fence
to break through or leap.

Leaping and bowing.

These poems were written between 1993 and 1998 in Sri Lanka and Canada.

"The Story" is for Akash and Mrs Mishra.
"House on a Red Cliff" is for Shaan and Pradip.
"Last Ink" is for Robin Blaser.

Some of the poems appeared in the following magazines: *Salmagundi, The Malahat Review, Antaeus, The London Review of Books, DoubleTake, The Threepenny Review, Granta, The New Yorker, The Arts Magazine* (Singapore), and the anthology *Writing Home*. "The Great Tree" was printed as a broadside by Outlaw Press in Victoria. Many thanks to all the editors.

I would like to thank Manel Fonseka, Kamlesh Mishra, Senake Bandaranayake, Anjalendran, Tissa Abeysekara, Dominic Sansoni, Milo Beach, and Ellen Seligman for their help at various stages during the writing of this book.

Some information in "The Great Tree" was drawn from *From Concept to Context—Approaches to Asian and Islamic Calligraphy*, an exhibition catalogue published by the Freer Gallery of Art, Smithsonian Institution, Washington, D.C., in 1986. A phrase in "A Gentleman Compares His Virtue to a Piece of Jade" was taken from *A History of Private Life* (vol. 1), published by Belknap Press, Harvard University

Press. A line from Van Morrison's song "Cypress Avenue" appears in "The Nine Sentiments." The image on the false-title page is an example of rock art, possibly a variation of a letter of the alphabet, found at Rajagalkanda in Sri Lanka. It appears in Senake Bandaranayake's book *Rock and Wall Paintings of Sri Lanka* (Lakehouse Bookshop, 1986). With thanks to the authors of these texts.

The jacket photograph, circa 1935, is by Lionel Wendt and is used with the kind permission of the Lionel Wendt Foundation, Colombo, Sri Lanka.

The epigraph on the dedication page is by Robert Louis Stevenson, from *A Child's Garden of Verses*.

Some of the traditions and marginalia of classical Sanskrit poetry and Tamil love poetry exist in the poem sequence "The Nine Sentiments." In Indian love poetry, the nine sentiments are romantic/erotic, humorous, pathetic, angry, heroic, fearful, disgustful, amazed, and peaceful. Corresponding to these are the aesthetic emotional experiences, which are called rasas, or flavours.

Certain words may need explanation: *parampara* literally means "from generation to generation." A *dagoba* is a Sri Lankan term for a stupa.

A NOTE ABOUT THE AUTHOR

Michael Ondaatje, poet and novelist, lives in Toronto, Canada. He is the author of the novels *In the Skin of a Lion* and *The English Patient*, a selected poems, *The Cinnamon Peeler*, and a memoir, *Running in the Family*. A complete list of his books will be found at the beginning of this volume.

A NOTE ON THE TYPE

The text of this book was set in a typeface called Aldus, designed by the celebrated typographer Hermann Zapf in 1952–1953. Based on the classical proportion of the popular Palatino type family, Aldus was originally adapted for Linotype composition as a slightly lighter version that would read better in smaller sizes.

Hermann Zapf was born in Nuremberg, Germany, in 1918. He has created many other well-known typefaces including Comenius, Hunt Roman, Marconi, Melior, Michelangelo, Optima, Saphir, Sistina, Zapf Book, and Zapf Chancery.

Typesetting by McClelland & Stewart, Toronto
Printed and bound by Quebecor Printing, Fairfield, Pennsylvania
Text designed by Sharmila Mohammed